# Kitchen & Bathroom Planning Guidelines with Access Standards

# Kitchen & Bathroom Planning Guidelines with Access Standards

National Kitchen & Bath Association

WILEY

John Wiley & Sons, Inc.

2012 *International Residential Code*. Washington, D.C.: International Code Council, 2011. Reprinted with permission. www.iccsafe.org

ICC A117.1 – 2009, *Accessible and Usable Buildings and Facilities*. Washington, D.C.: International Code Council, 2010. Reprinted with permission. www.iccsafe.org

This book is printed on acid-free paper. ∞

National Kitchen & Bath Association

687 Willow Grove Street

Hackettstown, NJ 07840

Phone: 800-THE-NKBA (800-843-6522)

Fax: 908-852-1695

Website: NKBA.org

For general information on our other products and services, or technical support, please contact our Customer Care Department within the United States at 800-762-2974, outside the United States at 317-572-3993 or fax 317-572-4002.

Wiley publishes in a variety of print and electronic formats and by print-on-demand. Some material included with standard print versions of this book may not be included in e-books or in print-on-demand. If this book refers to media such as a CD or DVD that is not included in the version you purchased, you may download this material at http://booksupport.wiley.com.

For more information about Wiley products, visit our Web site at http://www.wiley.com.

Library of Congress Cataloging-in-Publication Data:

978-1-118-34748-5 (pbk); 978-1-118-35088-1 (ebk); 978-1-118-35089-8 (ebk); 978-1-118-35193-2 (ebk); 978-1-118-35194-9 (ebk); 978-1-118-35195-6 (ebk)

Printed in the United States of America

10   9   8   7   6   5

# Contents

# Bathroom Planning Guidelines

# The NKBA

The National Kitchen & Bath Association (NKBA) is a leading nonprofit trade association dedicated to the advancement of the kitchen and bath industry. Since its inception nearly 50 years ago, the NKBA has maintained its leadership status of excellence and professionalism by providing education, certification, and the tools needed for success in the industry. NKBA Professional Development and Certification are the gold standard in the kitchen and bath industry. The NKBA offers professional development courses and levels of certification for all stages of an individual's career. The NKBA also offers networking opportunities and professional development training at over 70 chapters across North America.

## NKBA Learning & Development

NKBA Learning & Development provides kitchen and bath professionals convenient educational courses to enhance their careers. The NKBA offers Professional Development opportunities through in-person courses, virtual instructor-led training, eLearning, seminars, and conferences. The NKBA courses are aligned to specific industry segments such as designers, builders, installers, manufacturers, dealers, and more. Industry professionals can easily determine which courses are appropriate for their segment by viewing the course descriptions on the NKBA web site, NKBA.org. The NKBA also has more than 50 Accredited and Supported Programs in colleges and universities across North America that specialize in kitchen and bath design.

## NKBA Certification

NKBA Certification is based on in-depth testing, education, and industry experience allowing consumers to know that their designer's professional skills have been independently evaluated and tested. The NKBA certified professional members are committed to improving those skills by meeting continuing education and professional development requirements.

There are three levels of NKBA Certification for designers: Associate Kitchen & Bath Designer (AKBD®), Certified Kitchen Designer (CKD®) or Certified Bath Designer (CBD®), and Certified Master Kitchen & Bath Designer (CMKBD®). In addition, the NKBA offers education and testing for non-design-industry professionals to establish expertise and credibility as trade partners to certified designers through the Certified Kitchen & Bath Professional (CKBP®) certification.

# Methodology/Overview

The *NKBA Kitchen & Bath Planning Guidelines with Access Standards* is a collection of illustrations and planning suggestions to aid professionals in the safe and effective planning of kitchens and bathrooms. These guidelines are also included in NKBA Professional Resource Library *Kitchen Planning* and *Bath Planning* volumes. Designers and those interested in becoming kitchen and bath design professionals benefit by studying the complete body of knowledge found in the NKBA Professional Resource Library.

These flexible and easy-to-understand guidelines were developed under the guidance of the NKBA by a committee of professionals. The guidelines published in this booklet reflect a composite of the historical review, current industry environment, future trends, consumer lifestyles, new research, new building codes, and current industry practices.

The purpose of the guidelines is to serve as the basis for:

- Ensuring building code compliance.
- Recognizing the importance of consumer health, safety, and welfare in kitchen and bath design.
- Supporting sound kitchen and bath design practices.
- Testing core kitchen and bath competencies.
- Training designers in academic and educational programs.

# Kitchen Planning Guidelines with Access Standards

The National Kitchen & Bath Association developed the *Kitchen Planning Guidelines with Access Standards* to provide designers with good planning practices that consider the needs of a range of users.

The code references for the Kitchen Planning Guidelines are based on the analysis of the 2012 International Residential Code® (IRC®) and the International Plumbing Code®.

The code references for the Access Standards are based on ICC A117.1–2009 Accessible and Usable Buildings and Facilities.

Be sure to check local, state, and national laws that apply to your design and follow those legal requirements.

# Door/Entry

**Recommended:**
The clear opening of a doorway should be at least 32" (813 mm) wide. This would require a minimum 2' 10" (864 mm) door.

**Code Requirement:**
State or local codes may apply.

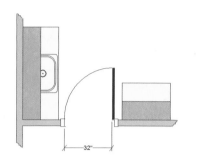

## Access Standard

**Recommended:**
The clear opening of a doorway should be at least 34" (864 mm). This would require a minimum 3' 0" (914 mm) door.

**ICC A117.1–2009 Reference:**
- Clear openings of doorways with swinging doors shall be measured between the face of door and stop, with the door open 90 degrees. (404.2.2)
- When a passage exceeds 24" (610 mm) in depth, the minimum clearance increases to 36" (914 mm). (404.2.2)

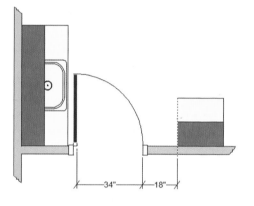

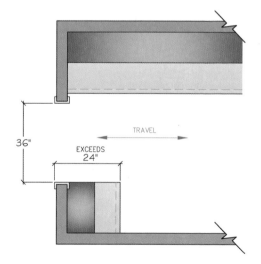

# Door Interference

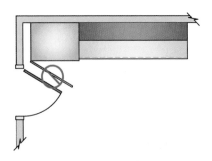

## Recommended:

No entry door should interfere with the safe operation of appliances, nor should appliance doors interfere with one another.

## Code Requirement:

State or local codes may apply.

## Access Standard

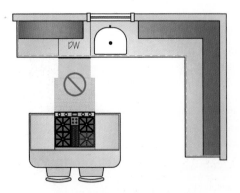

## Recommended:

In addition, the door area should include clear floor space for maneuvering, which varies according to the type of door and direction of approach.

## ICC A117.1–2009 Reference:

- For a standard hinged door, the clearance on the pull side of the door should be the door width plus 18" × 60" (457 mm × 1524 mm). (404.2.3)
- The clearance on the push side of the door should be the door width by 48" (1219 mm). (404.2.3)

FRONT APPROACH TO SWING DOORS (ACCESS STANDARD 2)

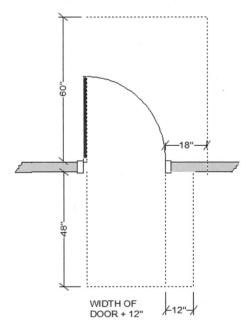

3

# Distance between Work Centers

**Recommended:**

In a kitchen with three work centers,* the sum of the three traveled distances should total no more than 26' (7.9 m), with no single leg of the triangle measuring less than 4' (1.2 m) or more than 9' (2.7 m).

When the kitchen plan includes more than three primary appliance/work centers, each additional travel distance to another appliance/work center should measure no less than 4' (1.2 m) nor more than 9' (2.7 m).

Each leg is measured from the center-front of the appliance/sink.

No work triangle leg intersects an island/peninsula or other obstacle by more than 12" (305 mm).

*A major appliance and its surrounding landing/work area form a work center. The distances between the three primary work centers (cooking surface, cleanup/prep sink, and refrigeration storage) form a work triangle.*

**Code Requirement:**

State or local codes may apply.

## Access Standard

**Recommended:**

Kitchen guideline recommendation meets Access Standard.

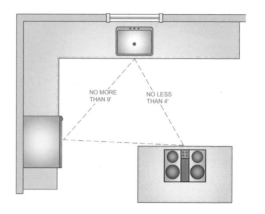

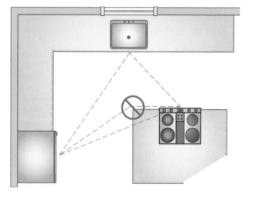

## Separating Work Centers

**Recommended:**
A full-height, full-depth, tall obstacle* should not separate two primary work centers.

A properly recessed tall corner unit will not interrupt the workflow and is acceptable.

*Examples of a full-height obstacle are a tall oven cabinet, tall pantry cabinet, and refrigerator.*

**Code Requirement:**
State or local codes may apply.

### Access Standard

**Recommended:**
Kitchen guideline recommendation meets Access Standard.

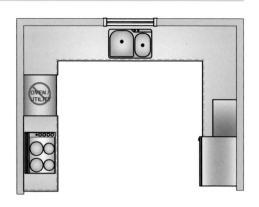

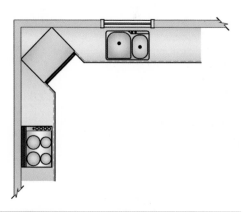

## Work Triangle Traffic

**Recommended:**
No major traffic patterns should cross through the basic work triangle.

**Code Requirement:**
State or local codes may apply.

### Access Standard

**Recommended:**
Kitchen guideline recommendation meets Access Standard.

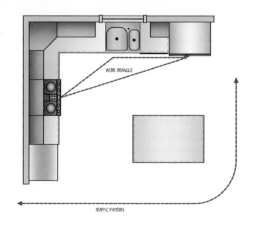

5

# Work Aisle

### Recommended:

The width of a work aisle should be at least 42" (1067 mm) for one cook and at least 48" (1219 mm) for multiple cooks. Measure between the counter frontage, tall cabinets, and/or appliances.

### Code Requirement:

State or local codes may apply.

## Access Standard

### Recommended:

Kitchen guideline recommendation meets Access Standard recommendation. See Code References for specific applications.

### ICC A117.1–2009 Reference:

A clear floor space of at least 30" × 48" (762 mm × 1219 mm) should be provided at each kitchen appliance. Clear floor spaces can overlap. (305.3, 804.5)

- In a U-shaped kitchen, plan a minimum clearance of 60" (1524 mm) between opposing arms. (804.2, 1003.12)
- Include a wheelchair turning space with a diameter of at least 60" (1524 mm), which can include knee* and toe** clearances. (304.3)
- A wheelchair turning space could utilize a T-shaped clear space, which is a 60" (1524 mm) square with two 12"

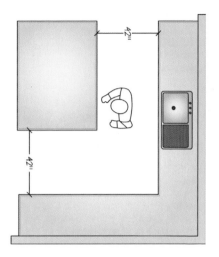

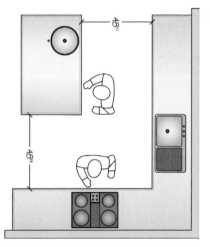

30" x 48"
CLEAR FLOOR SPACES AND
KNEE SPACES MAY OVERLAP

wide × 24" (305 mm × 610 mm) deep areas removed from the corners of the square. This leaves a minimum 36" (914 mm) wide base and two 36" (914 mm) wide arms. T-shaped wheelchair turning spaces can include knee and toe clearances. (304.3)

*\*Knee clearance must be 30" (762 mm) wide (36" [914 mm] to use as part of the T-turn) and maintain a 27" (686 mm) high clear space under the cabinet, counter, or sink. At 27" (686 mm) AFF, the depth must be a minimum 8" (203 mm). At 9" (229 mm) AFF, the depth must be a minimum 11" (279 mm). The space from 9" (229 mm) to the floor is considered toe clearance and must be a minimum of 17" (432 mm) and a maximum of 25" (635 mm).*

*\*\*Toe clearance space under a cabinet or appliance is between the floor and 9" (229 mm) above the floor. Where toe clearance is required as part of a clear floor space, the toe clearance should extend 17" (432 mm) minimum beneath the element. (306.2)*

**Code Requirement:**
State or local codes may apply.

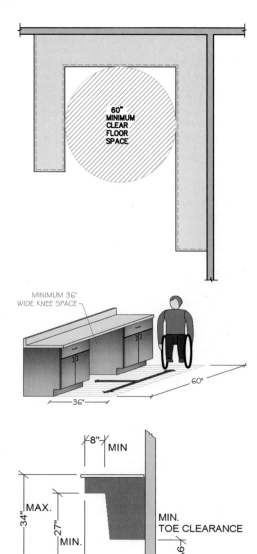

# Walkway

**Recommended:**
The width of a walkway should be at least 36" (914 mm).

**Code Requirement:**
State or local codes may apply.

# Access Standard

**Recommended:**
If two walkways are perpendicular to each other, one walkway should be at least 42" (1067 mm) wide.

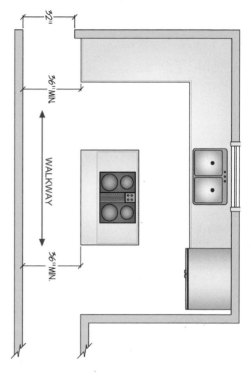

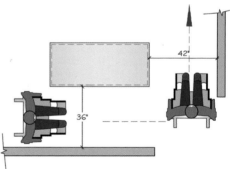

# Traffic Clearance at Seating

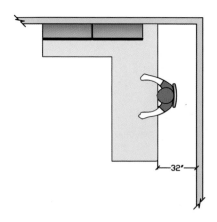

**Recommended:**

In a seating area where no traffic passes behind a seated diner, allow 32" (813 mm) of clearance from the counter/ table edge to any wall or other obstruction behind the seating area.

**a.** If traffic passes behind the seated diner, allow at least 36" (914 mm) to edge past.

**b.** If traffic passes behind the seated diner, allow at least 44" (1118 mm) to walk past.

**Code Requirement:**

State or local codes may apply.

## Access Standard

**Recommended:**

In a seating area where no traffic passes behind a seated diner, allow 36" (914 mm) of clearance from the counter/ table edge to any wall or other obstruction behind the seating area.

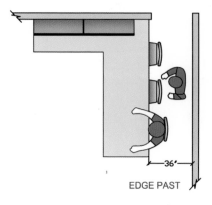

EDGE PAST

If traffic passes behind the seated diner, plan a minimum of 60" (1524 mm) to allow passage for a person in a wheelchair. This will be impacted by the depth of the knee space.

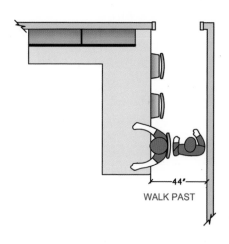

WALK PAST

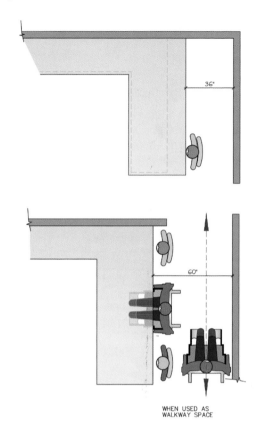

WHEN USED AS
WALKWAY SPACE

## KITCHEN PLANNING GUIDELINE 9

# Seating Clearance

**Recommended:**
Kitchen seating areas should
incorporate at least the
following clearances:

**a.** 30″ (762 mm) high tables/
counters: allow a 24″ wide ×
18″ deep (610 mm × 457 mm)
knee space for each seated
diner and at least 18″ × (457
mm) of clear knee space.

10

**b.** 36" (914 mm) high counters: allow a 24" wide × 15" deep (610 mm × 381m) knee space for each seated diner and at least 15" (381 mm) of clear knee space.

**c.** 42" (1067 mm) high counters: allow a 24" wide × 12" deep (610 mm × 305 mm) knee space for each seated diner and 12" (305 mm) of clear knee space.

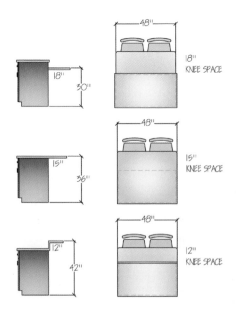

**Code Requirement:**
State or local codes may apply.

## Access Standard

**Recommended:**
Kitchen seating areas should be 28"–34" (711 mm–864 mm) high × 30"–36" (762 mm–914 mm) wide × 17"–25" (432 mm–635 mm) deep to better accommodate people of various sizes or those using a mobility aid.

Recommended minimum size for a knee space at a table or counter is 36" wide × 27" high × 17" deep (914 mm wide × 686 mm high × 432 mm deep).

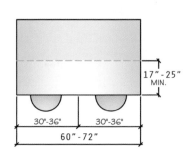

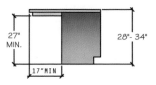

11

# Cleanup/Prep Sink Placement

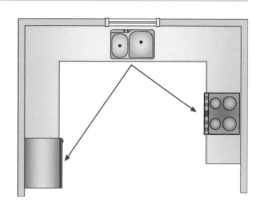

### Recommended:
If a kitchen has only one sink, locate it adjacent to or across from the cooking surface and refrigerator.

### Code Requirement:
State or local codes may apply.

## Access Standard

### Recommended:
Plan knee spaces at the sink to allow for a seated user. Recommended minimum size for a knee space is 36" wide × 27" high × 8" deep (914 mm × 686 mm × 203 mm), increasing to 17" (432 mm) deep in the toe space, which extends 9" (229 mm) from the floor. Insulation for exposed pipes should be provided.

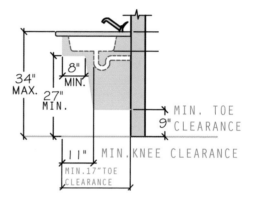

### ICC A117.1–2009 Reference:
- The sink should be no more than 34" (864 mm) high or adjustable between 29" and 36" (737 mm and 914 mm). (1003.12.4.2)
- Exposed water supply and drainpipes under sinks should be insulated or otherwise configured to protect against contact. There should be no sharp or abrasive surfaces under sinks. (1003.12.4.4)

# Cleanup/Prep Sink Landing Area

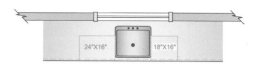

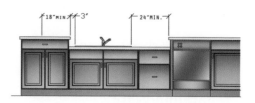

### Recommended:

Include at least a 24" (610 mm) wide landing area* to one side of the sink and at least an 18" (457 mm) wide landing area on the other side.

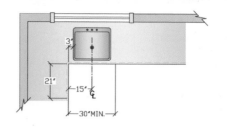

If all of the countertop at the sink is not the same height, then plan a 24" (610 mm) landing area on one side of the sink and 3" (76 mm) of countertop frontage on the other side, both at the same height as the sink.

The 24" (610 mm) of recommended landing area can be met by 3" (76 mm) of countertop frontage from the edge of the sink to the inside corner of the countertop if no more than 21" (533 mm) of countertop frontage is available on the return.

*Landing area is measured as countertop frontage adjacent to a sink and/or an appliance. The countertop must be at least 16" (406 mm) deep and must be 28" to 45" (711 mm to 1143 mm) above the finished floor to qualify.*

### Code Requirement:

State or local codes may apply.

## Access Standard

**Recommended:**
For a parallel approach for a person using a wheelchair, allow a minimum of 24" (610 mm) of countertop frontage from the centerline of the sink to the returning counter.

### KITCHEN PLANNING GUIDELINE 12

# Preparation/Work Area

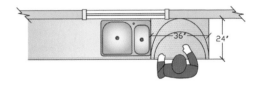

**Recommended:**
Include a section of continuous countertop at least 36" wide × 24" deep (914 mm × 610 mm) immediately next to a sink for a primary preparation/work area.

**Code Requirement:**
State or local codes may apply.

## Access Standard

**Recommended:**
A section of continuous countertop at least 30" (762 mm) wide with a permanent or adaptable knee space should be included somewhere in the kitchen.

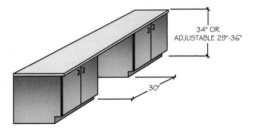

See Access Standard 6 for knee clearance specifications.

**ICC A117.1–2009 Reference:**
- In a kitchen, there should be at least one 30" (762 mm) wide section of counter, 34" (864 mm) high maximum

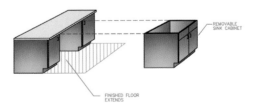

or adjustable from 29" to
36" (737 mm to 914 mm).
Cabinetry can be added
under the work surface,
provided it can be removed or
altered without removal or
replacement of the work
surface, and provided the
finished floor extends under
the cabinet. (1003.12.3)

## KITCHEN PLANNING GUIDELINE 13

# Dishwasher Placement

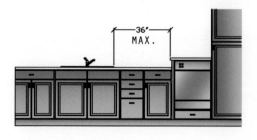

**Recommended:**
Locate nearest edge of the
primary dishwasher within 36"
(914 mm) of the nearest edge of
a cleanup/prep sink.

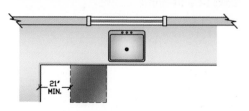

Provide at least 21"* (533 mm)
of standing space between the
edge of the dishwasher and
countertop frontage, appliances
and/or cabinets, which are
placed at a right angle to the
dishwasher.

*In a diagonal installation, the 21"
(533 mm) is measured from the
center of the sink to the edge of the
dishwasher door in an open position.*

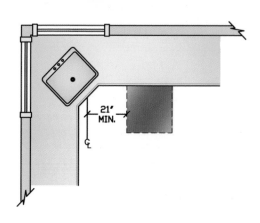

**Code Requirement:**
State or local codes may apply.

## Access Standard

**Recommended:**
Raise dishwasher 6" to 12"
(152 mm to 305 mm) when it

can be planned with appropriate landing areas at the same height as the sink.

**ICC A117.1–2009 Reference:**

- A clear floor space of at least 30" × 48" (762 mm × 1219 mm) should be positioned adjacent to the dishwasher door. The dishwasher door in the open position should not obstruct the clear floor space for the dishwasher or the sink. (1003.12.5.3)

KITCHEN PLANNING GUIDELINE 14

# Waste Receptacles

**Recommended:**
Include at least two waste receptacles. Locate one near each of the cleanup/prep sink(s) and a second for recycling either in the kitchen or nearby.

**Code Requirement:**
State or local codes may apply.

## Access Standard

**Recommended:**
Kitchen guideline recommendation meets Access Standard.

## Auxiliary Sink

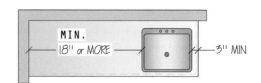

**Recommended:**
At least 3" (76 mm) of countertop frontage should be provided on one side of the auxiliary sink, and 18" (457 mm) of countertop frontage on the other side, both at the same height as the sink.

**Code Requirement:**
State or local codes may apply.

### Access Standard

**Recommended:**
Plan a knee space at, or adjacent to, the auxiliary sink.

See Access Standard 6 for knee clearance specifications.

## Refrigerator Landing Area

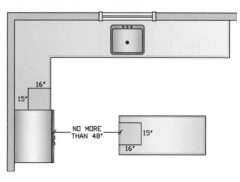

**Recommended:**
Include at least:

**a.** 15" (381 mm) of landing area on the handle side of the refrigerator, or

**b.** 15" (381 mm) of landing area on either side of a side-by-side refrigerator, or

**c.** 15" (381 mm) of landing area which is no more than 48" (1219 mm) across from the front of the refrigerator, or

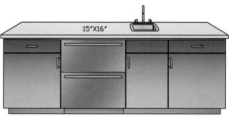

**d.** 15" (381 mm) of landing area above or adjacent to any undercounter-style refrigeration appliance.

**Code Requirement:**
State or local codes may apply.

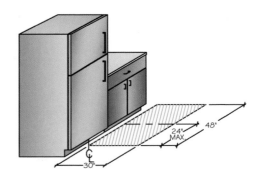

## Access Standard

**Recommended:**
See Code Reference

### ICC A117.1–2009 Reference:

- A clear floor space of 30" × 48" (762 mm × 1219 mm) should be positioned for a parallel approach to the refrigerator/freezer with the centerline of the clear floor space offset on the handle side 24" (610 mm) maximum from the centerline of the appliance. (804.6.6, 1003.12.6)

---

**KITCHEN PLANNING GUIDELINE 17**

# Cooking Surface Landing Area

**Recommended:**
Include a minimum of 12" (305 mm) of landing area on one side of a cooking surface and 15" (381 mm) on the other side.

If the cooking surface is at a different countertop height than the rest of the kitchen, then the 12" and 15" (305 mm and 381 mm) landing areas must be at the same height as the cooking surface.

For safety reasons, in an island or peninsula situation, the countertop should also extend a minimum of 9" (229 mm) behind the cooking surface if the counter height is the same as the surface-cooking appliance.

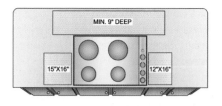

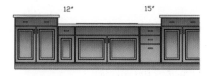

- For an enclosed configuration, a reduction of clearances shall be in accordance with the appliance manufacturer's instructions or per local codes. (This may not provide adequate landing area.) (IRC M 1901.2) (IRC E 4101.2)

**Code Requirement:**
State or local codes may apply.

## Access Standard

**Recommended:**
Lower the cooktop to 34" (864 mm) maximum height and create a knee space beneath the appliance.

See Access Standard 6 for knee clearance specifications.

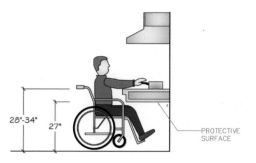

**ICC A117.1–2009 Reference:**
- When a forward-approach clear floor space is provided at the cooktop, it should provide knee and toe clearance, and the underside of the cooktop should be insulated or otherwise configured to prevent burns,

abrasions, or electric shock. (1003.12.5.4)

- Where the clear floor space is positioned for a parallel approach, the clear floor space shall be centered on the appliance. (1003.12.5.4)
- The location of cooktop controls should not require reaching across burners. (1003.12.5.4)

## KITCHEN PLANNING GUIDELINE 18

# Cooking Surface Clearance

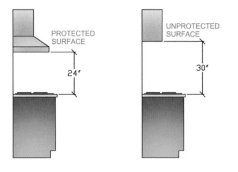

**Recommended:**
Allow 24" (610 mm) of clearance between the cooking surface and a protected noncombustible surface above it.

**Code Requirement:**

- At least 30" (762 mm) of clearance is required between the cooking surface and an unprotected/combustible surface above it. (IRC M 1901.1) (IRC G 244705)
- If a microwave/hood combination is used above the cooking surface, then the manufacturer's specifications should be followed. (IRC M 1504.1) (IRC G 2447.5)

Refer to manufacturer's specifications or local building codes for other considerations.

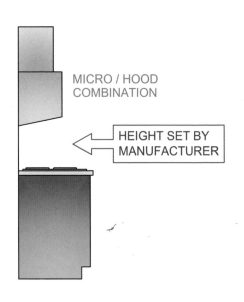

MICRO / HOOD COMBINATION

HEIGHT SET BY MANUFACTURER

## Access Standard

**Recommended:**
Kitchen guideline
recommendation meets Access
Standard.

# Cooking Surface Ventilation

**Recommended:**
Provide a correctly sized,
ducted ventilation system for all
cooking surface appliances. The
recommended minimum is 150
cubic feet per minute (cfm).

MINIMUM 150 CFM

**Code Requirement:**
- Manufacturer's installation
  instructions and
  specifications must be
  followed. (IRC G 2407.1, IRC G
  2447.1, IRC E 4101.2)
- The minimum required
  exhaust rate for a ducted hood
  is 100 cfm and must be ducted
  to the outside. (IRC M 1507.3)
- Exhaust hood systems capable
  of exhausting in excess of 400
  cfm shall be provided with
  makeup air at a rate
  approximately equal to the
  exhaust air rate. Such makeup
  air systems shall be equipped
  with a means of closure and
  shall be automatically
  controlled to start and operate
  simultaneously with the
  exhaust system. (IRC M 1503.4)
- Refer to local codes for more
  restricted requirements.

## Access Standard

### Recommended:

Ventilation controls should be placed 15" to 44" (381 mm to 1118 mm) above the floor, operable with minimal effort, easy to read, and with minimal noise pollution. Plan storage of frequently used items 15" to 48" (381 mm to 1219 mm) above the floor.

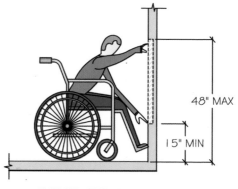

48" MAX

15" MIN

UNOBSTRUCTED FORWARD REACH

### ICC A117.1–2009 Reference:

- Operable parts should be operable with one hand and not require tight grasping, pinching, or twisting of the wrist. The force required to activate operable parts should be 5 pounds (2 kg) maximum. (309.4)

- Where a forward or side reach is unobstructed, the high reach should be 48" (1219 mm) maximum, and the low reach should be 15" (381 mm) minimum above the floor. (308.2.1, 308.3.1)

- Where a forward or reach is obstructed by a 20" to 25" (508 mm to 635 mm) deep counter, the high reach should be 44" (1118 mm) maximum. (308.2.2)

- When a side reach is obstructed by a 10" to 24" (254 mm to 610 mm) counter, the high reach should be 46" (1168 mm). (308.3.2)

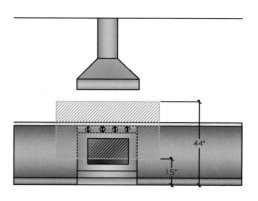

44"

15"

VENTILATION CONTROLS
WITHIN 15"–44"
REACH CONTROL

# Cooking Surface Safety

**Recommended:**

**a.** Do not locate the cooking surface under an operable window.

**b.** Window treatments above the cooking surface should not use flammable materials.

**c.** A fire extinguisher should be located near the exit of the kitchen away from cooking equipment.

**d.** Commercial cooking appliances are not to be installed in residential kitchens. (IRC M 1901.3) (IRC G 2447.2)

**Code Requirement:**
State or local codes may apply.

## Access Standard

**Recommended:**
Place fire extinguisher between 15" and 48" (381 mm and 1219 mm) off the finished floor.

Select cooking appliances with the controls located so that there is no need to reach across burners to operate. (1003.12.5.4.4)

**UNACCEPTABLE**

GLASS BLOCK

**ACCEPTABLE**

# Microwave Oven Placement

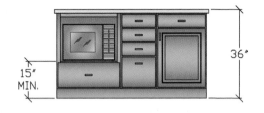

**Recommended:**

Locate the microwave oven after considering the user's height and abilities. The ideal location for the bottom of the microwave is 3" (76 mm) below the principle user's shoulder but no more than 54" (1372 mm) above the floor.

If the microwave oven is placed below the countertop the oven bottom must be at least 15" (381 mm) off the finished floor.

**Code Requirement:**

State or local codes may apply.

## Access Standard

**Recommended:**

Locate the microwave controls no higher than 46" to 48" (1168 mm to 1219 mm) depending on approach and reach range. (See Access Standard 19.)

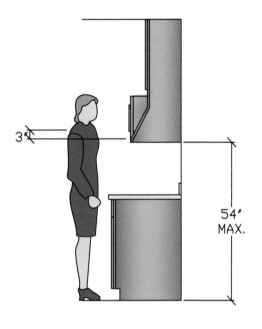

# Microwave Landing Area

**Recommended:**
Provide at least a 15" (381 mm) landing area above, below, or adjacent to the handle side of a microwave oven.

**Code Requirement:**
State or local codes may apply.

## Access Standard

**Recommended:**
Provide landing area in front of or immediately adjacent to the handle side of the microwave.

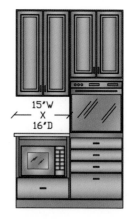

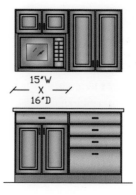

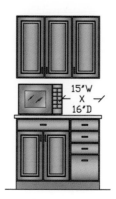

## Oven Landing Area

### Recommended:
Include at least a 15" (381 mm) landing area next to or above the oven.

At least a 15" (381 mm) landing area that is not more than 48" (1219 mm) across from the oven is acceptable if the appliance does not open into a walkway.

### Code Requirement:
State or local codes may apply.

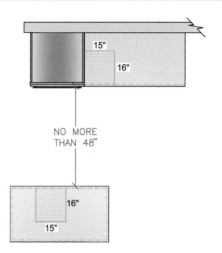

## Access Standard

### Recommended:
See Code reference.

### ICC A117.1–2009 Reference:
- For side-opening ovens, the door latch side should be next to a countertop. (1003.12.5.5.2)

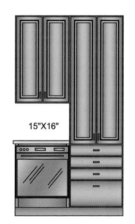

# Combining Landing Areas

**Recommended:**
If two landing areas are adjacent to one another, determine a new minimum for the two adjoining spaces by taking the longer of the two landing area requirements and adding 12″ (305 mm).

**Code Requirement:**
State or local codes may apply.

## Access Standard

**Recommended:**
Kitchen guideline recommendation meets Access Standard.

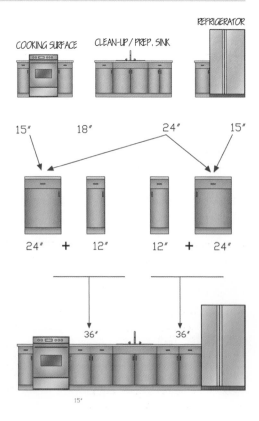

# Countertop Space

**Recommended:**
A total of 158″ (4013 mm) of countertop frontage, 24″ (610 mm) deep, with at least 15″ (381 mm) of clearance above, is needed to accommodate all uses, including landing area, preparation/work area, and storage.

Built-in appliance garages extending to the countertop can be counted towards the total countertop frontage recommendation, but they may interfere with the landing areas.

**Code Requirement:**
State or local codes may apply.

## Access Standard

**Recommended:**
At least two work-counter heights should be offered in the kitchen, with one 28" to 36" (711 mm to 914 mm) above the finished floor and the other 36" to 45" (914 mm to 1143 mm) above the finished floor.

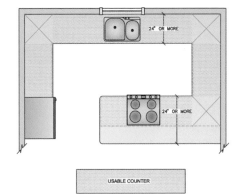

# Countertop Edges

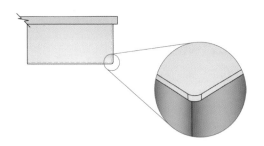

**Recommended:**
Specify clipped or round corners rather than sharp edges on all counters.

**Code Requirement:**
State or local codes may apply.

## Access Standard

**Recommended:**
Kitchen guideline recommendation meets Access Standard.

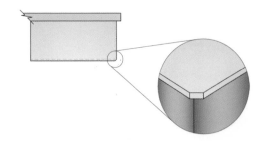

# Storage

**Recommended:**
The total shelf/drawer frontage* is:

a. 1400" (35,560 mm) for a small kitchen (less than 150 square feet) (14 m²);

b. 1700" (43,180 mm) for a medium kitchen (151 to 350 square feet) (14 m² to 32.5 m²);

c. 2000" (50,800 mm) for a large kitchen (greater than 350 square feet) (32.5 m²).

### Shelf/Drawer Frontage in Inches

|         | Small | Medium | Large |
|---------|-------|--------|-------|
| Wall    | 300"  | 360"   | 360"  |
| Base    | 520"  | 615"   | 660"  |
| Drawer  | 360"  | 400"   | 525   |
| Pantry  | 180"  | 230"   | 310"  |
| Misc.   | 40"   | 95"    | 145"  |

### Shelf/Drawer Frontage in Millimeters

|         | Small    | Medium    | Large     |
|---------|----------|-----------|-----------|
| Wall    | 7620 mm  | 9144 mm   | 9144 mm   |
| Base    | 1320 mm  | 15621 mm  | 16764 mm  |
| Drawer  | 9144 mm  | 10160 mm  | 13335 mm  |
| Pantry  | 4572 mm  | 5842 mm   | 7874 mm   |
| Misc.   | 1016 mm  | 2413 mm   | 3683 mm   |

The totals for wall, base, drawer, and pantry shelf/drawer frontage can be adjusted upward or downward as long as the recommended total stays the same.

Do not apply more than the recommended amount of storage in the miscellaneous category to meet the total frontage recommendation.

Storage areas that are more than 84" (2134 mm) above the floor must be counted in the miscellaneous category.

*Shelf and drawer frontage is determined by multiplying the cabinet size by the number and depth of the shelves or drawers in the cabinet, using the following formula: Cabinet width in inches × number of shelf and drawers × cabinet depth in feet (or fraction thereof) = Shelf and Drawer Frontage.*

*Storage/organizing items can enhance the functional capacity of wall, base, drawer, and pantry storage and should be selected to meet user needs.*

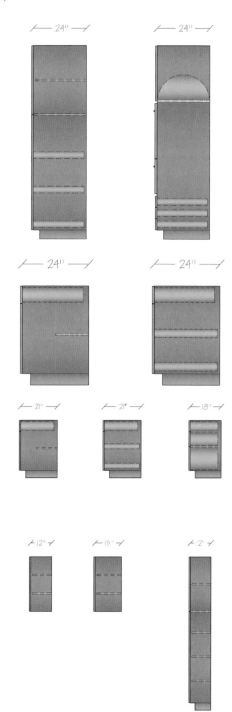

**Code Requirement:**
State or local codes may apply.

## Access Standard

**Recommended:**
See Guideline 19.

### ICC A117.1–2009 Reference:

- Where a forward or side reach is unobstructed, the high reach should be 48" (1219 mm) maximum and the low reach should be 15" (381 mm) minimum above the floor. (A117.1 308.2.1, 308.3.1)

- Where a 20" to 25" (508 mm to 635 mm) deep counter obstructs a forward reach, the high reach should be 44" (1118 mm) maximum. (A117.1 308.2.2)

- Where a 10" to 24" (254 mm to 610 mm) counter obstructs a side reach, the high reach should be 46" (1168 mm) maximum. (A117.1308.3.2)

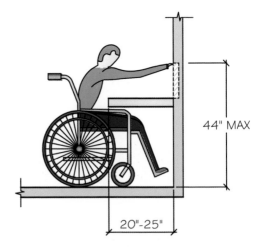

OBSTRUCTED HIGH FORWARD REACH

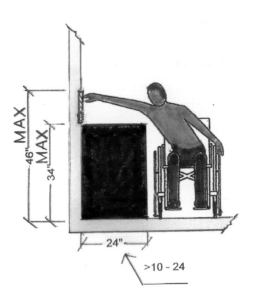

# Storage at Cleanup/ Prep Sink

### Recommended:

Of the total recommended wall, base, drawer, and pantry shelf/ drawer frontage, the following should be located within 72" (1829 mm) of the centerline of the main cleanup/prep sink:

**a.** At least 400" (10,160 mm) for a small kitchen.
b. At least 480" (12,192 mm) for a medium kitchen.
**c.** At least 560" (14,224 mm) for a large kitchen.

### Code Requirement:

State or local codes may apply.

## Access Standard

### Recommended:

Plan storage of frequently used items 15" to 48" (381 mm to 1219 mm) above the floor.

### ICC A117.1–2009 Reference:

- See Access Standard 19 for reach specifications.

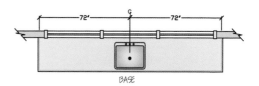

BASE

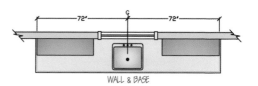

WALL & BASE

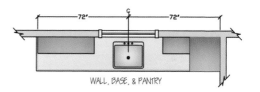

WALL, BASE, & PANTRY

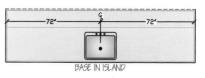

BASE IN ISLAND

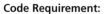

OPEN WALL STORAGE

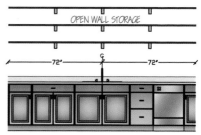

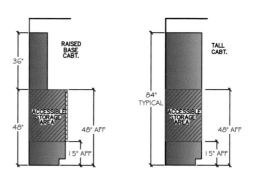

# Corner Cabinet Storage

**Recommended:**
At least one corner cabinet should include a functional storage device.

This guideline does not apply if there are no corner cabinets.

**Code Requirement:**
State or local codes may apply.

## Access Standard

**Recommended:**
Kitchen guideline recommendation meets Access Standard.

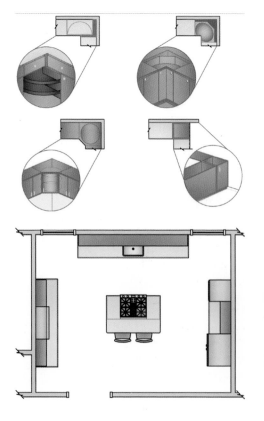

# Electrical Receptacles

**Code Requirement:**
• GFCI (Ground-fault circuit-interrupter) protection is required on all receptacles servicing countertop surfaces within the kitchen. (IRC E 3902.6)

Refer to IRC E 3901.3 through E 3901.4.5 for receptacle placement and locations.

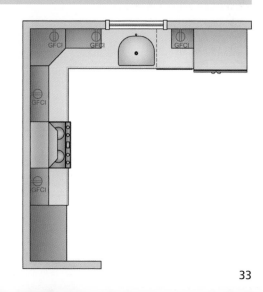

## Access Standard

**Recommended:**
See Code Reference.

**Code Reference:**
See Access Standard 19 for
reach and control specifications.

# Lighting

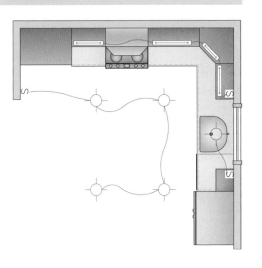

**Recommended:**
In addition to general lighting
required by code, every work
surface should be well
illuminated by appropriate task
lighting.

**Code Requirement:**
- At least one wall switch–
  controlled light must be
  provided. Switch must be
  placed at the entrance. (IRC E
  3903.2)
- Window/skylight area, equal
  to at least 8% of the total
  square footage of the kitchen,
  or a total living space that
  includes a kitchen, is required.
  (IRC R 303.1, IRC R 303.2)

## Access Standard

**Recommended:**
Lighting should be from multiple
sources and adjustable.

**ICC A117.1–2009 Reference:**
- See Access Standard 19 for
  reach and control
  specifications.

# Bathroom Planning Guidelines with Access Standards

The National Kitchen & Bath Association developed the Bathroom Planning Guidelines with Access Standards to provide designers with good planning practices that consider the needs of a range of users.

The code references for the Bathroom Planning Guidelines are based on the analysis of the 2012 International Residential Code® (IRC®) and the International Plumbing Code®.

The code references for the Access Standards are based on ICC A117.1–2009 Accessible and Usable Buildings and Facilities.

Be sure to check local, state, and national laws that apply to your design and follow those legal requirements.

# Door/Entry

### Recommended:

The clear opening of a doorway should be at least 32″ (813 mm). This would require a minimum 2′ 10″ (864 mm) door.

If the existing structure precludes changing the opening, then a minimum 2′ 0″ (610 mm) door is allowable.

### Code Requirement:

State or local codes may apply.

## Access Standard

### Recommended:

The clear opening of a doorway should be at least 34″ (864 mm). This would require a minimum 3′ 0″ (914 mm) door.

### ICC A117.1–2009 Reference:

- Clear openings of doorways with swinging doors shall be measured between the face of door and stop, with the door open 90 degrees. (404.2)
- When the depth of a passage exceeds 24″ (610 mm), the minimum clear opening increases to 36″ (914 mm). (404.2.2)

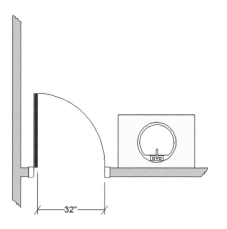

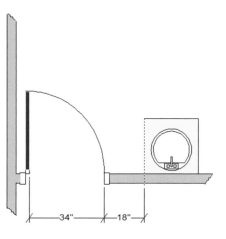

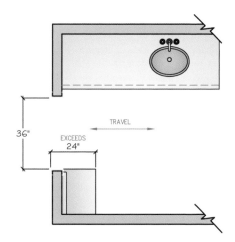

# Door Interference

### Recommended:
See Code Reference.

### Code Requirement:
- No entry or fixture doors should interfere with one another and/or the safe use of the fixtures or cabinets. (IRC P 2705.1)

## Access Standard

### Recommended:
The door area should include clear floor space for maneuvering, which varies according to the type of door and the direction of approach.

### ICC A117.1–2009 Reference:
- For a standard hinged door, the minimum clearance on the pull side of the door should be the width of the door plus 18″ by 60″ (457 mm × 1524 mm). (404.2.3)
- The minimum clearance on the push side of the door should be the width of the door plus 12″ × 48″ (305 mm × 1219 mm). (404.2.3)

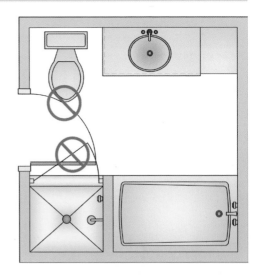

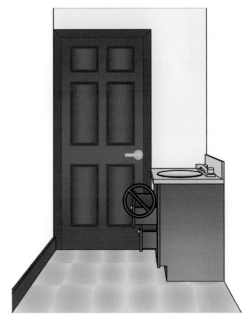

FRONT APPROACH TO SWING
DOORS

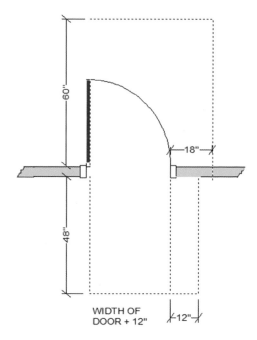

60"

48"

—18"—

WIDTH OF
DOOR + 12"

12"

## BATHROOM PLANNING GUIDELINE 3

# Ceiling Height

**Recommended:**
See Code Requirement.

**Code Requirement:**
- Bathrooms shall have a minimum floor to ceiling height of 80" (2032 mm) over the fixture and at the front clearance area for fixtures. (IRC 305.1)
- A shower or tub equipped with a shower head shall have a minimum floor to ceiling height of 80" (2032 mm)

above a minimum area 30″ × 30″ (762 mm × 762 mm) at the shower head. (IRC 305.1)

### Access Standard

**Recommended:**
Bathroom Guideline code requirement meets Access Standard.

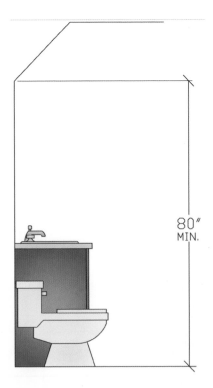

80″ MIN.

---

## BATHROOM PLANNING GUIDELINE 4

# Clear Space

**Recommended:**
Plan a clear floor space of at least 30″ (762 mm) from the front edge of all fixtures (e.g., lavatory, toilet, bidet, tub, and shower) to any opposite bath fixture, wall or obstacle.

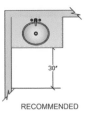

RECOMMENDED

RECOMMENDED

**Code Requirement:**
• A minimum space of at least 21″ (533 mm) must be planned in front of lavatory, toilet, bidet, and tub. (IRC P 2705.1.5) (IRC R 307.1)

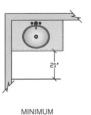

MINIMUM

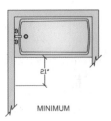

MINIMUM

- A minimum space of at least 24" (610 mm) must be planned in front of a shower entry. (IRC R 307.1)

## Access Standard

### Recommended:

Plan a minimum clear floor space of 30" × 48" (762 mm × 1219 mm) centered at each fixture, plus space for maneuvering including approach and turning for a person using a wheelchair.

Plan a knee space at the lavatory or work space to allow for a front approach for a seated user. Recommended minimum size of a knee space is 36" wide × 27" high × 8" deep (914 mm × 686 mm × 203 mm), increasing to 17" (432 mm) deep in the toe space, which extends 9" (229 mm) from the floor. Insulation for exposed pipes should be provided.

Consider the user's method of transfer to the toilet to plan a clear space to fit the user's needs.

### ICC A117.1–2009 Reference:

- A clear floor space of at least 30" × 48" (762 mm × 1219 mm) must be provided at each fixture. Clear spaces can overlap. (305.3)
- Include a wheelchair turning space with a diameter of at

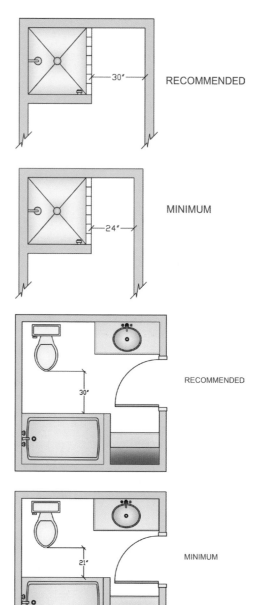

RECOMMENDED

MINIMUM

RECOMMENDED

MINIMUM

least 60″ (1524 mm), which can include knee* and toe** clearances. (304.3.0)

- A wheelchair turning space could utilize a T-shaped space, which is a 60″ (1524 mm) square with two 12″ wide × 24″ deep (305 mm × 610 mm) areas removed from two corners of the square. This leaves a minimum 36″ (914 mm) wide base and two 36″ (914 mm) wide arms. T-shaped wheelchair turning spaces can include knee* and toe** clearances on one arm. (304.3.2)

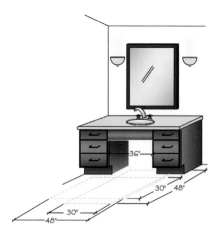

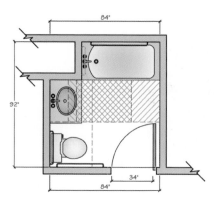

*Knee clearance must be a minimum 30″ (762 mm) wide (36″ [914 mm] to use as part of the T-turn) and maintain a 27″ (686 mm) high clear space under the cabinet, counter, or sink. At 27″ (686 mm), Above Finished Floor (AFF) the depth must be a minimum 8″ (203 mm). At 9″ (229 mm) AFF, the depth must be a minimum of 11″ (279 mm). The space from 9″ (229 mm) to the floor is considered toe clearance and must be a minimum of 17″ (432 mm) and a maximum of 25″ (635 mm). (306.3)

FIXTURE CLEAR FLOOR SPACE

**Toe clearance space under a cabinet or fixture is between the floor and 9″ (635 mm) above the floor. Where toe clearance is required as part of a clear floor space, the toe clearance should extend 17″ (432 mm) minimum beneath the element. (306.2.3)

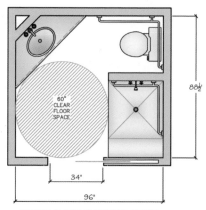

WHEELCHAIR TURNING SPACE

**Grooming**

- The clear 30″ × 48″ (762 mm × 1219 mm) floor space should be centered on the lavatory. (606.2, 1004.11.3)

**Bathing and Showering**

- Clearance in front of bathtubs should extend the length of the bathtub and be at least 30″ (762 mm) wide. (607.2)
- When a permanent seat is provided at the head of the bathtub, the clearance should extend a minimum of 12″ (305 mm) beyond the wall at the head end of the bathtub. (607.2)
- The clearance in front of the transfer-type shower* compartment should be at least 48″ (1219 mm) long measured from the control wall and 36″ (914 mm) wide. (608.2)
- The clearance in front of a roll-in-type shower** compartment should be at least 60″ (1524 mm) long next to the open face of the shower compartment and 30″ (762 mm) wide. (608.2.2)

*A transfer shower, 36″ × 36″ (914 mm × 914 mm), provides support to a standing person or one who can stand to transfer.

**A roll-in shower is a waterproof area large enough for a person in a wheelchair to remain in the chair to shower. A preferred minimum size

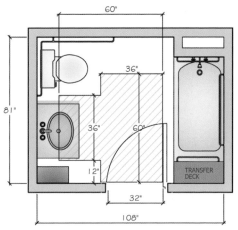

MINIMUM 36″ x 36″ x 60″
SPACE FOR T-TURNS

KNEE STANDARD (ACCESS STANDARD 4—ANSI)

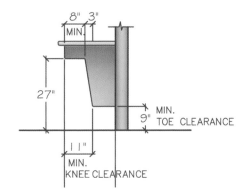

*for a roll-in shower is 36″—42″ × 60″ (914 mm to 1067 mm × 1524 mm).*

### Toileting

- When both a parallel and a forward approach to the toilet are provided, the clearance should be at least 56″ (1422 mm) measured perpendicular from the rear wall, and 60″ (1524 mm) measured perpendicular from the sidewall. No other fixture or obstruction should be within the clearance area. (604.3, 1002.11.2.4)

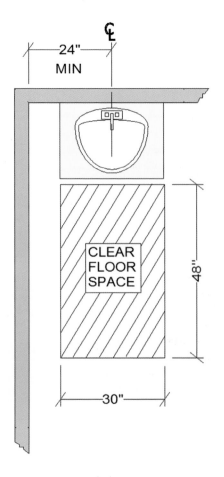

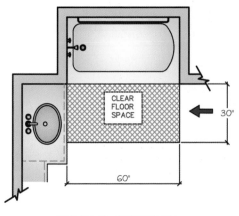

PARALLEL APPROACH

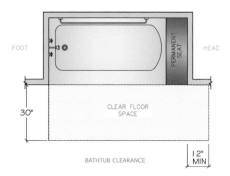

FOOT    PERMANENT SEAT    HEAD

30"

CLEAR FLOOR SPACE

12" MIN

BATHTUB CLEARANCE

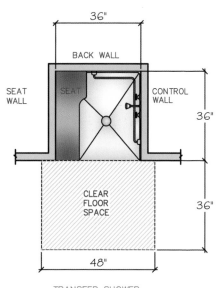

36"

BACK WALL

SEAT WALL    SEAT    CONTROL WALL

36"

CLEAR FLOOR SPACE

36"

48"

TRANSFER SHOWER

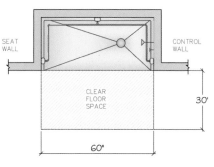

BACK WALL

SEAT WALL    CONTROL WALL

CLEAR FLOOR SPACE

30'

60"

ROLL-IN SHOWER

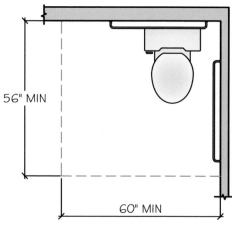

56" MIN

60" MIN

TOILET APPROACH

## BATHROOM PLANNING GUIDELINE 5

### Single-Lavatory Placement

**Recommended:**
The distance from the centerline of the lavatory to the sidewall/tall obstacle should be at least 20" (508 mm).

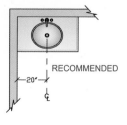

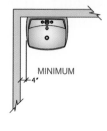

• The minimum distance between a wall and the edge of a freestanding or wall-hung lavatory is 4" (102 mm).

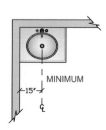

**Code Requirement:**
• The minimum distance from the centerline of the lavatory to a wall is 15" (381 mm). (IRC P2705)

## Access Standard

### ICC A117.1–2009 Reference:
- To assure a clear floor space (30″ × 48″) (762 mm × 1219 mm), the lavatory must be a minimum 24″ (610 mm) from the wall.
  (A117.1, 1004.11.3)

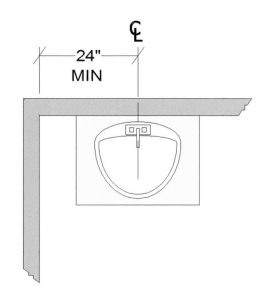

---

**BATHROOM PLANNING GUIDELINE 6**

# Double-Lavatory Placement

**Recommended:**
The distance between the centerlines of two lavatories should be at least 36″ (914 mm). The minimum distance between the edges of two freestanding or wall-hung lavatories is 4″ (102 mm).

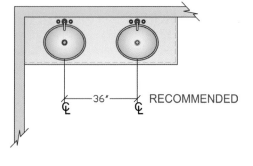

**Code Requirement:**
- The minimum distance between the centerlines of two lavatories should be at least 30″ (762 mm). (IRC P 2705)

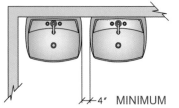

## Access Standard

**Recommended:**
Bathroom guideline recommendation meets Access Standard.

# Lavatory/Vanity Height

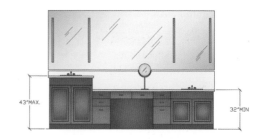

**Recommended:**
The height for a lavatory varies between 32″ and 43″ (813 mm and 1092 mm) to fit the user.

**Code Requirement:**
State or local codes may apply.

## Access Standard

**Recommended:**
Lavatory controls should be within the user's reach and operable with minimal effort.

**ICC A117.1–2009 Reference:**
- The front of the lavatory sink should be no more than 34″ (864 mm) above the floor, measured to the higher of the fixture or counter surface.
(606.3)
- Lavatory controls should be operable with one hand and not require tight grasping, pinching, or twisting of the wrist. (309.4)

# Counter

**Recommended:**
Specify clipped or round corners rather than sharp edges on all counters.

**Code Requirements:**
State or local codes may apply.

## Access Standard

**Recommended:**
Bathroom guideline
recommendation meets Access
Standard.

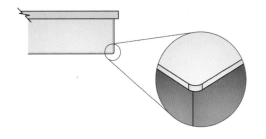

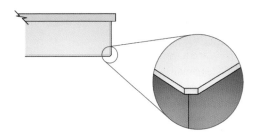

---

## BATHROOM PLANNING GUIDELINE 9

# Shower Size

**Recommended:**
The interior shower size is at
least 36″ × 36″ (914 mm
× 914 mm).

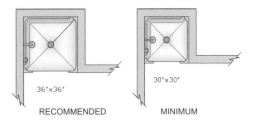

36′×36′

RECOMMENDED

30′×30′

MINIMUM

**Code Requirement:**
- The minimum interior shower
  size is 30″ × 30″ (762 mm
  × 762 mm) or 900 square
  inches (5806 cm²), in which
  a disc of 30″ (762 mm) in
  diameter must fit.
  (IRC P 2708.1)

## Access Standard

**Recommended:**
- Plan either a transfer or a
  roll-in shower.
- Roll-in shower entries: For a
  60″ (1524 mm) deep

shower, a 32″ (813 mm) wide entry is adequate. For a 42″ (1067 mm) deep shower, the entry must be at least 36″ (914 mm) wide to allow for turning space.

### ICC A117.1–2009 Reference:

- Transfer-type shower compartments must have an inside finished dimension of 36″ × 36″ (914 mm × 914 mm), and have a minimum of 36″ (914 mm) wide entry on the face of the shower compartment. A folding seat must be provided within the 36″ × 36″ (914 mm × 914 mm) area. (608)

- Roll-in-type shower compartments should have a minimum inside finished dimension of at least 30″ (762 mm) wide by 60″ (1524 mm) deep, and have a minimum of a 60″ (1524 mm) wide entry on the face of the shower compartment. (608.2.2)

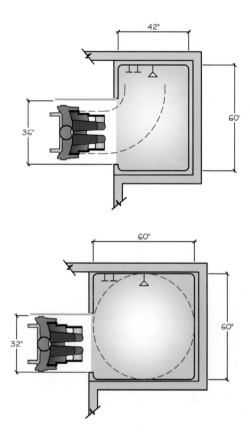

TRANSFER TYPE SHOWER (ACCESS STANDARD 9–ANSI)

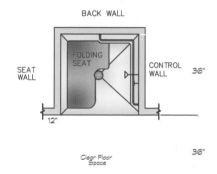

ROLL—IN SHOWER (ACCESS STANDARD 9 — ANSI)

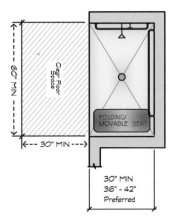

60" MIN

Clear Floor Space

FOLDING/ MOVABLE SEAT

30" MIN

30" MIN
36" - 42"
Preferred

## BATHROOM PLANNING GUIDELINE 10

# Tub/Shower Controls

### Recommended:

**a.** The shower controls should be accessible from both inside and outside the shower spray and be located between 38″ and 48″ (965 mm and 1219 mm) above the floor depending on user's height.

**b.** The tub controls should be accessible from both inside and outside the tub and be located between the rim of the bathtub and 33″ (838 mm) above the floor.

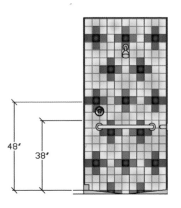

48'

38'

### Code Requirement:

State or local codes may apply.

## Access Standard

### Recommended:

Controls should be offset toward the room and easy to

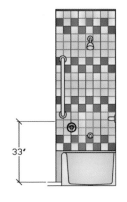

33'

grasp, as with lever or loop handles (a and b).

Hot and cold should be identified with red and blue indicators.

Provide a handheld spray at a height accessible to the user (b).

### ICC A117.1–2009 Reference:

- Tub/shower controls must be operable with one hand and not require tight grasping. (309.4)
- Controls must be on an end wall of the bathtub, between the rim and grab bar, and between the open side of the bathtub and the midpoint of the width of the tub. (607.5) (a)
- In transfer-type shower compartments, controls and the handheld shower head should be on the sidewall adjacent to the seat, between 38″ and 48″ (965 mm and 1219 mm) above the shower floor, within 15″ (381 mm) of the centerline of the control wall toward the shower opening. (b) (608.4.1)
- Controls in roll-in showers should be above the grab bar, but no higher than 48″ (1219 mm) above the shower floor and minimum 16″ (406 mm), maximum 27″ (686 mm) from the end wall behind the seat. (608.4.2) (c)

a.

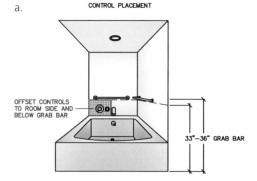

CONTROL PLACEMENT

OFFSET CONTROLS TO ROOM SIDE AND BELOW GRAB BAR

33″–36″ GRAB BAR

b.

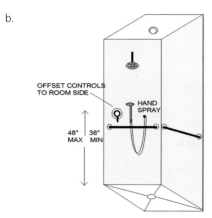

OFFSET CONTROLS TO ROOM SIDE

HAND SPRAY

48″ MAX   38″ MIN

c.

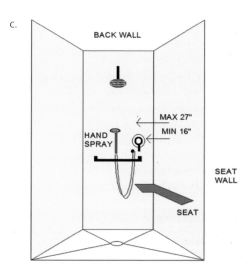

BACK WALL

MAX 27″
MIN 16″

HAND SPRAY

SEAT WALL

SEAT

ROLL-IN SHOWER

- A handheld spray unit must
  be provided with a hose at
  least 59" (1499 mm) long that
  can be used as a fixed
  showerhead and as a
  handheld shower. If an
  adjustable height showerhead
  mounted on a vertical bar is
  used, the bar should not
  obstruct the use of the grab
  bars. (608.5)

## BATHROOM PLANNING GUIDELINE 11

# Water Temperature Safety

**Recommended:**
See below.

**Code Requirement:**
Shower and tub/shower control
valves must be one of the
following:

- Pressure balanced.
- Thermostatic mixing.
- Combination pressure
  balance/thermostatic mixing
  valve types. (IRC P 2708.3)
  (IRC M 1507.4)

The valve must have a high limit
stop to prevent water
temperatures above 120°F
(49°C). (IRC P 2708.3)

Hot water delivered to bathtubs
and whirlpool bathtubs shall be

limited to a temperature of not
more than 120°F (49°C).
(IRC P 2713.3)

Hot water delivered to bidets
shall be limited to no more than
110°F (43°C). (IRC P 2721.2)

### Access Standard

**Recommended:**
Bathroom guideline code
requirement meets Access
Standard. (607.8, 608.8)

## BATHROOM PLANNING GUIDELINE 12

# Shower/Tub Seat

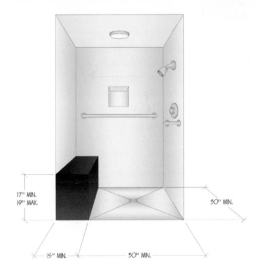

**Recommended:**
Plan a seat within the shower
that is 17"–19" (432 mm × 483
mm) above the shower floor
and 15" (381 mm) deep.

**Code Requirement:**
• Shower seat must not
  infringe on the minimum
  interior size of the shower
  (900 square inches) (5806
  cm²). (IRC P 2708.1)

### Access Standard

**Recommended:**
Plan a seat in the shower and/
or bathtub to fit the parameters
of the space and the needs of
the user.

### ICC A117.1–2009 Reference:

- A removable in-tub seat should be at least 15″ to 16″ (381 mm to 406 mm) deep and capable of secure placement. (610.2)
- A permanent tub seat should be at least 15″ (381 mm) deep and positioned at the head end of the bathtub. The top of the seat should be between 17″ and 19″ (432 mm and 483 mm) above the bathroom floor. (610.2)
- A shower seat should be 15″ to 16″ deep (381 mm to 406 mm) and 17″ to 19″ (432 mm and 483 mm) above the shower floor (to top of the seat). The seat should extend from the back wall to a point within 3″ (76 mm) of the entry. In a transfer shower, the seat should be on the wall opposite the control wall. In a roll-in shower, the fold down seat should be on a wall, extending from the control wall to the shower entry. (ICC 608, 610)
- The materials and installation of the shower and/or bathtub seat must support a minimum of 250 (113 kg) pounds of pressure. (610.4)

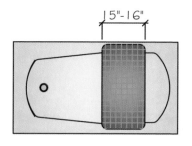

(a) REMOVEABLE IN—TUB SEAT

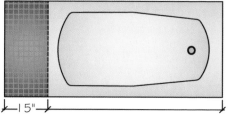

PERMANENT SEAT

# Tub/Shower Surround

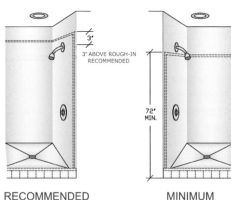

RECOMMENDED          MINIMUM

3" ABOVE ROUGH-IN RECOMMENDED

72" MIN.

### Recommended:

The wall area above a tub or shower pan should be covered in a waterproof material extending at least 3" (76 mm) above the showerhead rough in.

### Code Requirement:

- The wall area above a tub or shower pan must be covered in a waterproof material to a height of not less than 72" (1829 mm) above the finished floor. (IRC R 307.2)

## Access Standard

### Recommended:

Bathroom guideline recommendation meets Access Standard.

# Grab Bars

### Recommended:

Plan grab bars to facilitate access to and maneuvering within the tub and shower areas.

Tub and shower walls should be prepared (reinforced) at time of construction to allow for installation of grab bars to support a static load of 250 lbs (113 kg).

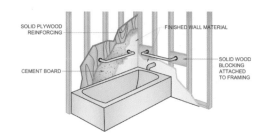

SOLID PLYWOOD REINFORCING

FINISHED WALL MATERIAL

CEMENT BOARD

SOLID WOOD BLOCKING ATTACHED TO FRAMING

Grab bars should be placed at 33″ to 36″ (838 mm to 914 mm) above the floor.

Grab bars must be $1\frac{1}{4}$″ to 2″ (32 mm to 60 mm) in diameter and extend $1\frac{1}{2}$″ (38 mm) from the wall.

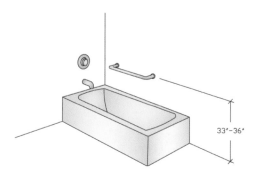

33′–36′

## Access Standard

### Recommended:

Walls throughout the bathroom should be prepared (reinforced) at time of construction to allow for installation of grab bars to support a minimum of 250 lbs. (113 kg) of force in any direction.

Grab bars should be placed according to the needs and height of the user, particularly near the tub/shower and the toilet.

### ICC A117.1–2009 Reference:

Grab bars should be installed at the tub, shower, and toilet according to the following:

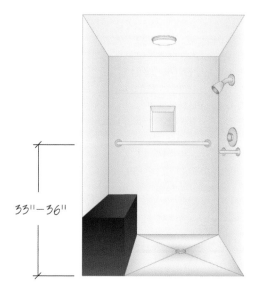

33″–36″

- Bathtubs with permanent seats: Two horizontal grab bars (a1) should be provided on the back wall, one 33″ to 36″ (838 mm to 914 mm) above the floor and the other 8″ to 10″ (203 mm to 254 mm) above the rim of the bathtub (a2). Each grab bar should be no more than 15″ (381 mm) from the head end wall or 12″ (305 mm) from the control end wall. A

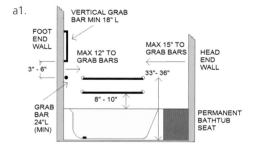

a1.

VERTICAL GRAB BAR MIN 18" L

FOOT END WALL

MAX 12" TO GRAB BARS

MAX 15" TO GRAB BARS

HEAD END WALL

3" - 6"

33"- 36"

8" - 10"

GRAB BAR 24"L (MIN)

PERMANENT BATHTUB SEAT

grab bar 24″ (610 mm) long should be provided on the control end wall at the front edge of the bathtub. A vertical grab bar minimum 18″ (457 mm) shall be placed 3″–6″ (76 mm to 152 mm) above and 4″ (102 mm) maximum from the front edge of the horizontal bar. (607.4.1)

- Bathtubs without permanent seats: Two horizontal grab bars should be provided on the back wall, one 33″ to 36″ (838 mm to 914 mm) above the floor and the other 8″ to 10″ (203 mm to 254 mm) above the rim of the bathtub (a3). Each grab bar should be at least 24″ (610 mm) long and no more than 24″ (610 mm) from the head end wall or 12″ (305 mm) from the control end wall. A horizontal grab bar 24″ (610 mm) long should be provided on the foot end wall at the front edge of the bathtub. A horizontal grab bar 12″ (305 mm) minimum in length should be provided on the head end wall at the front edge of the bathtub. On the control wall, a vertical grab bar minimum 18″ (457 mm) shall be placed 3″ to 6″ (76 mm to 152 mm) above and 4″ (102 mm) maximum from the front edge of the horizontal. (a4). (607.4.2)

- Transfer-type showers: Grab bars should be mounted in a

a2.

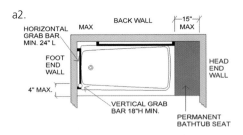

a3.

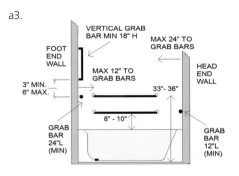

a4.

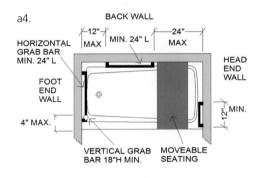

b.

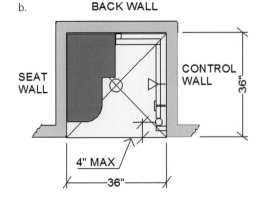

horizontal position, between 33" and 36" (838 mm and 914 mm) above the shower floor, across the control wall and on the back wall to a point 18" (457 mm) from the seat wall. A vertical grab bar minimum 18" (457 mm) shall be placed 3" to 6" (76 mm to 152 mm) above the horizontal bar and 4" (102 mm) maximum from the front edge of the shower. (608.3) (b)

- Roll-in type shower: Grab bars should be mounted in a horizontal position, between 33" and 36" (838 mm and 914 mm) above the floor, on all three walls of the shower. An exception is that there be no grab bar on the length of wall behind and for the length of the seat. Grab bars should be no more than 6" (152 mm) from each adjacent wall. (608.3.2) (c1, c2, and c3)

- Toilet: Grab bars should be provided on the rear wall and on the sidewall closest to the toilet 33" to 36" (838 mm to 914 mm) high. Sidewall grab bar should be at least 42" (1067 mm) long, located between 12" (305 mm) and 54" (1372 mm) from the rear wall. In addition, a vertical grab bar, 18" (457 mm) minimum length, shall be mounted with the bottom of the bar 39" to 41" (991 mm to 1041 mm) AFF and centerlined between 39" and 41" (991 mm and 1041 mm) from the rear

c1.
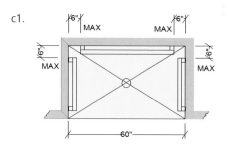

(A) STANDARD ROLL-IN-TYPE SHOWER

c2.
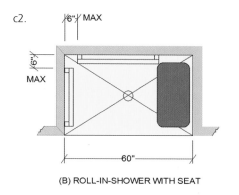

(B) ROLL-IN-SHOWER WITH SEAT

c3.
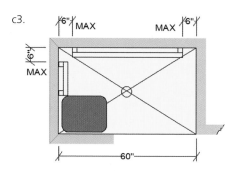

(C) ALTERNATE ROLL-IN-TYPE SHOWER

wall. The rear grab bar should be at least 24″ (610 mm) long, centered on the toilet. Where space permits, the bar should be at least 36″ (914 mm) long, with the additional length provided on the transfer side of the toilet. (604.5) (d1 and d2)

d1.

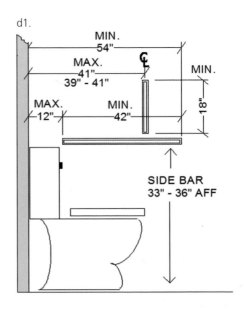

**SIDE WALL GRAB BARS FOR TOILET**

d2.

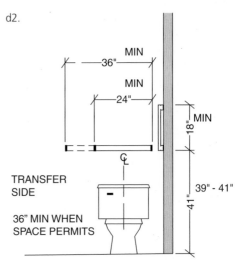

**REAR WALL GRAB BAR FOR TOILET**

# Glazing

**Recommended:**
See Code Requirement.

**Code Requirement:**
- Glass used in tub or shower enclosures (e.g., tub or shower door) or partitions must be tempered or an approved equal and must be permanently marked as such. (IRC R 308.1)
- If the tub or shower surround has glass windows or walls, the glazing must be tempered glass or approved equal when the bottom edge of glazing is less than 60" (1524 mm) above any standing or walking surface. (IRC R 308.4)
- Any glazing (e.g., windows or doors) whose bottom edge is less than 18" (457 mm) above the floor must be tempered glass or approved equal. (IRC R 308.4)

## Access Standard

**Recommended:**
Consider line of sight of user when planning height of bottom of glazing.

# Tub/Shower Door

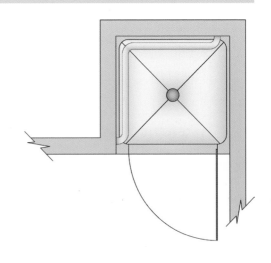

**Recommended:**
See Code Requirement.

**Code Requirement:**
Hinged shower doors shall open outward. (IRC P 2708.1)

## Access Standard

**Recommended:**
Minimize thresholds at the shower entry to no more than $\frac{1}{2}''$ (13 mm).

**ICC A117.1–2009 Requirement:**
• Shower compartment thresholds should be no more than $\frac{1}{4}''$ to $\frac{1}{2}''$ (6 mm to 13 mm) high.

Changes in level between $\frac{1}{4}''$ high and $\frac{1}{2}''$ (6 mm to 13 mm) high should be beveled with a slope not steeper than 1:2. (608.6.303)

# Steps

**Recommended:**
Steps should not be placed outside a tub.

If steps are used, a grab bar/handrail is mandatory.

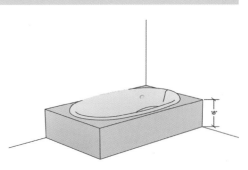

## Access Standard

**Recommended:**
Bathroom guideline recommendation meets Access Standard.

# Flooring

**Recommended:**
Slip-resistant surfaces should be specified for the general bath flooring, shower floors, and tub/shower bottoms.

**Code Requirement:**
State or local codes may apply.

## Access Standard

**Recommended:**
Bathroom guideline recommendation meets Access Standard.

# Equipment Access

**Recommended:**
See below.

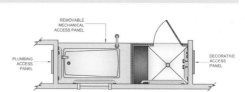

**Code Requirement:**
- All equipment, including access panels, must be installed as per manufacturers' specifications. (IRC P 2720.1)
- All manufacturers' instructions must be available for installers and inspectors and left for homeowners. (IRC P 2720.4)

## Access Standard

**Recommended:**
Equipment controls should be placed between 15″ and 48″ (381 mm and 1219 mm) above the finished floor.

---

**BATHROOM PLANNING GUIDELINE 20**

# Toilet/Bidet Placement

**Recommended:**
The distance from the centerline of toilet and/or bidet to any bath fixture, wall or other obstacle should be at least 18″ (457 mm).

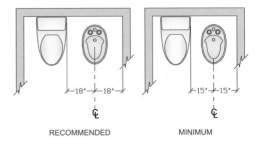

RECOMMENDED      MINIMUM

**Code Requirement:**
- A minimum distance of 15″ (381 mm) is required from the centerline of toilet and/or bidet to any bath fixture, wall, or other obstacle.
(IRC R 307.1, IRC P 2705.1)

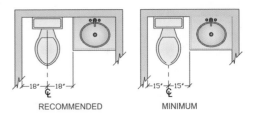

RECOMMENDED      MINIMUM

## Access Standard

**Recommended:**
Consider user height and ability when determining toilet height.

**ICC A117.1–2009 Reference:**
- The toilet should be centered 16″ to 18″ (406 mm to 457 mm) from a side wall. (1003.11.2.4)
- The toilet seat should be between 15″ and 19″ (381 mm and 483 mm) from the floor. (1003.11.2.4.5)

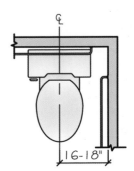

# Toilet Compartment

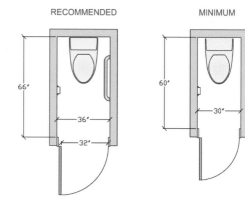

RECOMMENDED

MINIMUM

## Recommended:

The size for a separate toilet compartment should be at least 36″ × 66″ (914 mm × 1676 mm) with a swing-out or pocket door.

## Code Requirement:

- The minimum size for a separate toilet compartment is 30″ × 60″ (762 mm × 1524 mm). (IPC 405.3.1)

## Access Standard

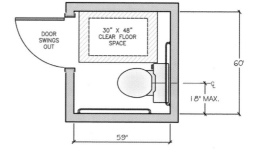

### Recommended:

To maximize access, provide privacy in the toileting area without using a separate compartment.

### ICC A117.1–2009 Reference:

- Wheelchair-accessible compartments should be at least 60″ (1524 mm) wide, measured perpendicular to the sidewall, and 56″ (1422 mm) deep for a wall-hung toilet and 59″ (1499 mm) deep for a floor-mounted toilet measured perpendicular to the rear wall. (604.7)

## Storage

**Recommended:**
Provide adequate, accessible storage for toiletries, bath linens, grooming, and general bathroom supplies at point of use.

**Code Requirement:**
State or local codes may apply.

## Access Standard

**Recommended:**
Plan storage of frequently used items between 15″ and 48″ (381 mm and 1219 mm) above the finished floor.

### ICC A117.1–2009 Reference:

- Where a forward or side reach is unobstructed, the high reach should be 48″ (1219 mm) maximum, and the low reach should be 15″ (381 mm) minimum above the floor. (308.2.1, 308.3.1)
- Where a forward or side reach is obstructed by a 20″ to 25″ (508 mm to 635 mm) deep counter, the high reach should be 44″ (1118 mm) maximum. (308.2.2, 308.3.2)
- Door/drawer pulls should be operable with one hand, require only a minimal amount of strength for operation, and should not require tight grasping. (309.4)

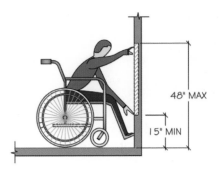

UNOBSTRUCTED FORWARD REACH

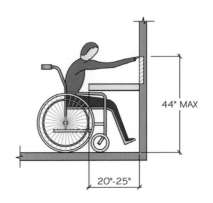

OBSTRUCTED HIGH FORWARD REACH

# Accessories

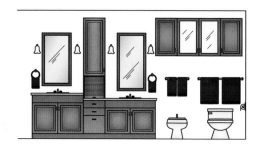

## Recommended:

**a.** Place a mirror above or near the lavatory at a height that takes the user's eye height into consideration.

**b.** The toilet paper holder should be located 8″ to 12″ (203 mm to 305 mm) in front of the edge of the toilet bowl, centered at 26″ (660 mm) above the floor.

**c.** Additional accessories, such as towel holders and soap dishes, should be conveniently located near all bath fixtures.

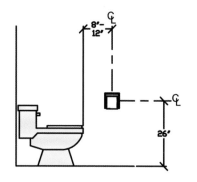

## Code Requirement:

State or local codes may apply.

## Access Standard

## Recommended:

**a.** Plan a full-height mirror to provide reflection at eye level, regardless of the user's height or stature.

**b.** See Code Reference on toilet paper placement.

**c.** Accessories should be placed between 15″ and 48″ (381 mm and 1219 mm) above the floor, and operable with a closed fist and with minimal effort.

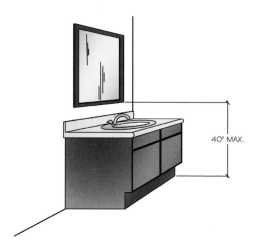

## ICC A117.1–2009 Reference:

• Mirrors above lavatories should have the bottom edge of the reflecting surface no more than 40″ (1016 mm) above the floor. (603.3)

- The toilet paper holder should be 24″–42″ (610 mm–1067 mm) off the rear wall and between 18″ and 48″ (457 mm and 1219 mm) above the floor with a clearance of at least $1\frac{1}{2}$″ (38 mm) below or 12″ (305 mm) above the grab bar. (604.7) (a + b)

See Access Standard 22 for reach specifications.

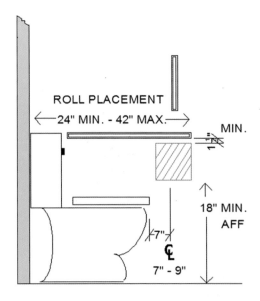

**ROLL PLACEMENT**
←24" MIN. - 42" MAX.→
$1\frac{1}{2}$" MIN.
18" MIN. AFF
7"
₵
7" - 9"

**(A) BELOW GRAB BAR**

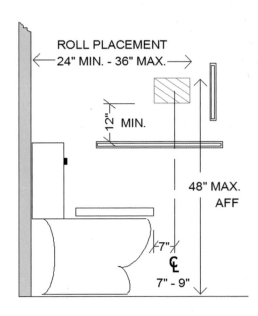

**ROLL PLACEMENT**
←24" MIN. - 36" MAX.→
12" MIN.
48" MAX. AFF
7"
₵
7" - 9"

**(B) ABOVE GRAB BAR**

# Electrical Receptacles

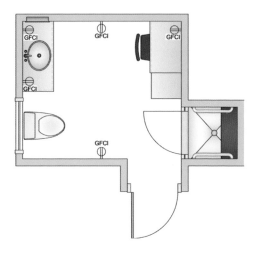

**Recommended:**

All GFCI receptacles should be located at electrical appliance points of use.

**Code Requirement:**

- At least one GFCI protected receptacle must be installed within 36" (914 mm) of the outside edge of the lavatory. (IRC E 3901.6)
- All receptacles must be protected by ground-fault circuit interrupters. (IRC 3902.1)
- A receptacle shall not be installed within or directly over a bathtub or shower stall. (IRC E 4002.11)
- Switches shall not be installed within wet locations in the tub or shower spaces or within reach while standing in the tub or shower unless installed as part of the listed tub or shower assembly. (IRC E 4001.7)

## Access Standard

**Recommended:**

See Code Reference.

**ICC A117.1–2009 Reference:**

See Access Standard 22 for specifications for placement within reach range.

# Lighting

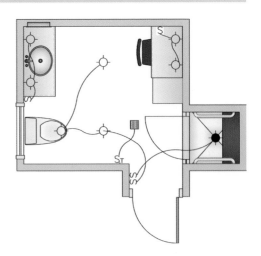

**Recommended:**

In addition to general lighting, task lighting should be provided for each functional area in the bathroom (e.g., grooming, showering).

**Code Requirement:**

- At least one wall switch–controlled light must be provided. Switch must be placed at the entrance of the bathroom. (IRC E 3903.2)
- All light fixtures installed within tub and shower spaces should be marked "suitable for damp/wet locations." (IRC E 4003.9, 4003.10)
- Hanging fixtures cannot be located within a zone of 3' (914 mm) horizontally and 8' (2438 mm) vertically from the top of the bathtub rim or shower stall threshold. (IRC E 4003.11)

## Access Standard

**Recommended:**

Task lighting at the vanity should be beside the mirror and at eye level, with the lamp not visible to the eye.

Lighting controls should be between 15" and 48" (381 mm and 1219 mm) above the floor and operable with a closed fist and with minimal effort.

## ICC A117.1–2009 Reference:

- Operable parts should be operable with one hand and not require tight grasping, pinching, or twisting of the wrist. The force required to activate operable parts should be 5 pounds (2 kg) maximum. (309.4)

See Access Standard 22 for specifications for reach range for controls.

## BATHROOM PLANNING GUIDELINE 26

# Ventilation

### Recommended:
Plan a mechanical exhaust system, vented to the outside, for each enclosed area.

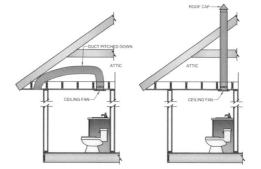

### Code Requirement:

- Minimum ventilation for the bathroom is to be a window of at least 3 square feet (0.27 m²) of which 50% is operable, or a mechanical ventilation system of at least 50 cubic feet (15,240 cubic mm) per minute (cfm) exhausted to the outside. (IRC R 303.3, IRC M 1507.2, IRC M 1507.3)

## Access Standard

### Recommended:
Ventilation controls should be placed 15" to 48" (381 mm to 1219 mm) above the floor,

operable with minimal effort, easy to read, and with minimal noise pollution.

**ICC A117.1–2009 Reference:**
See Access Standard 25 for operable controls.

See Access Standard 22 for reach range for controls.

## BATHROOM PLANNING GUIDELINE 27

# Heat

**Recommended:**
A supplemental heat source (e.g., heat lamp, toe kick heater, or floor heat) should be considered.

**Code Requirement:**
- All bathrooms should have an appropriate heat source to maintain a minimum room temperature of 68° Fahrenheit (20° Celsius). (IRC R 303.8)

HEAT LAMP     HEAT / FAN / LIGHT

RADIANT FLOOR SYSTEM

TOEKICK HEATER

WALL HEATER

## Access Standard

**Recommended:**
See Code Reference.

**ICC A117.1–2009 Reference:**
See Access Standard 25 for operable controls.

See Access Standard 22 for reach range for controls.

# Measurement Conversions

Commonly Used Measurements
for Landing Areas, Work Isles,
and Preparation Centers

|  9 | inches | = |  229 | millimeters |
| 12 | inches | = |  305 | millimeters |
| 15 | inches | = |  381 | millimeters |
| 18 | inches | = |  457 | millimeters |
| 21 | inches | = |  533 | millimeters |
| 24 | inches | = |  610 | millimeters |
| 36 | inches | = |  914 | millimeters |
| 42 | inches | = | 1067 | millimeters |
| 48 | inches | = | 1219 | millimeters |

*Note: Millimeter measurements shown
throughout this publication have been
rounded to the nearest whole number
when applicable.*

**Notes:**

**Notes:**

**Notes:**

**Notes:**

**Notes:**

**Notes:**

# Notes:

# Notes:

# Notes:

**Notes:**

# The NKBA Professional Resource Library

In order to apply the NKBA Kitchen & Bathroom Planning Guidelines with Access Standards to design projects in a holistic manner, read the NKBA's *Kitchen Planning, Second Edition* and *Bath Planning, Second Edition*, both published by John Wiley & Sons.

Using the Guidelines as a foundation, the infrastructure, environmental, electrical, and mechanical considerations of kitchen and bath planning are incorporated into these comprehensive reference books filled with drawings and photographs in full color. Historical and consumer trends, research on design and planning, sustainability and universal design are explained in an easy-to-read manner. *Kitchen Planning* and *Bath Planning* also include worksheets, checklists, and forms for assessing needs for each room.

Kitchen Planning and Bath Planning are part of the NKBA Professional Resource Library. This collection of books is being updated and expanded: visit www.wiley.com/go/nkba or www.nkba.org to see the latest available resources.

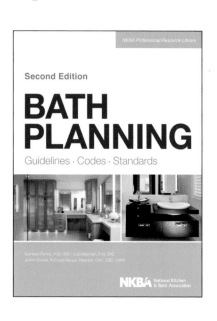

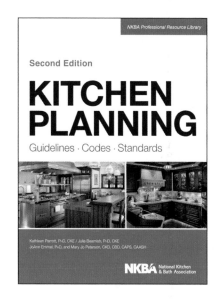